Emilie Roi

A Different Story

Emilie Roi

A Different Story

About a Danish Jewish Girl During World War Two

Translated from the Hebrew by Miriam Arad

Illustrations by Nitai Baruch

יד ושם
YAD VASHEM
THE WORLD HOLOCAUST REMEMBRANCE CENTER

THE INTERNATIONAL INSTITUTE FOR HOLOCAUST RESEARCH

Emilie Roi

Sipur Aher
Al Yalda Bedenia Hakvusha

Language and Production Editor: Leah Goldstein

P.O.B. 3477, Jerusalem 9103401, Israel
publications.marketing@yadvashem.org.il
First published in Hebrew by Hakibbutz Hameuchad, 1980
First English Edition published by Yad Vashem, 1990
New English Edition, 2018
Second printing, 2022

ISBN 978-965-308-547-3

Design: 2W design
Printed in Israel by Printiv Press, Jerusalem

For Talia, Giora, Itamar and Micha

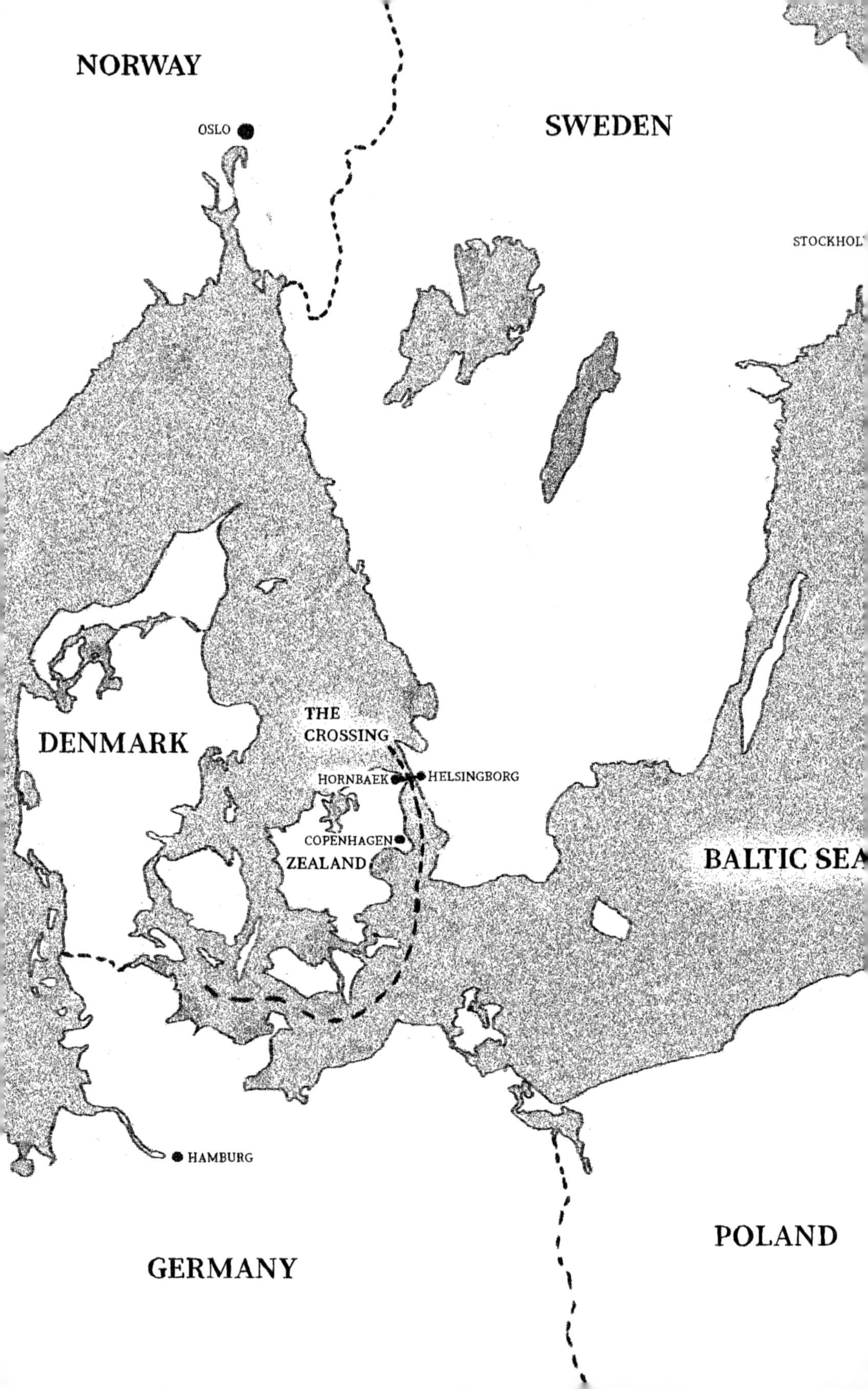
NORWAY
OSLO
SWEDEN
STOCKHOL
DENMARK
THE CROSSING
HORNBAEK
HELSINGBORG
COPENHAGEN
ZEALAND
BALTIC SEA
HAMBURG
POLAND
GERMANY

CONTENTS

PART ONE

TIMES PAST

I am sure you have heard about the Holocaust. Or maybe you have just heard the word, Holocaust, and you know it is something terrible. It is. It belongs to the days when the Nazis of Germany had conquered nearly all of Europe, killing many, many people, but above all, and most of all, killing Jews.

It was a fearful time.

And it makes the story of that time I want to tell you different, because it is a story with a happy ending. I think stories like that should always be told. Don't you?

About myself

First, I'll tell you about me. I was born in Denmark. Know where that is? Look at a map of Europe. Way up in the north, on top of Germany, there's a large peninsula, which looks a bit like a funny sort of head with a long nose. That's one part of Denmark. The other part is made up of a whole lot of islands, the biggest of which is called Zealand.

Zealand is very near two other countries that are even higher up north. On the map they look like a great tiger. Those are Sweden and Norway. Nearly all the Jews of Denmark live on Zealand, and that's where we lived, too.

We were a large family of eight children, and I was the youngest. Actually, we weren't eight, but seven, until our cousin came to live with us, and we all thought of him as a brother.

I looked very funny as a child. I was short and fat, with broad shoulders. My neck was short, too, and my head big, making it look as though it were stuck right on my chest.

Whenever I needed new clothes, my mother used to start worrying weeks ahead. She knew we would be dragging from one store to the next, but still not finding anything that would be right for me. It always ended up with me wearing clothes that my sisters had outgrown. They would be taken in a little here, let out a little there, and be "as good as new." Buying me shoes was even more of a challenge. Unlike the rest of me, my feet were long and narrow, and wouldn't fit into any shoes.

I had a broad face, a large chin, and droopy hair with never a curl in it – and curls were what I wanted more than anything. But what could I do if all I had were just two silly little pigtails, which seemed to grow out of my head right behind my ears?

I was born the year my grandma – my father's mother – died, so they named me after her: Esmeralda. I cried many tears on account of that name. Besides, I didn't want to be like my grandma at all. However, just as if to spite me, the grownups would take one look at my face and go all sloppy: "Isn't that child the very picture of her grandma!" It was a comfort that my own family, at least, found "Esmeralda" too much for them, and called me Maya for short.

Only at school did the name continue to haunt me. Whenever the teacher got mad at me, she'd say: "You are not living up to your name, Esmeralda!" The whole class would burst out laughing, and I would freeze in my chair and fix my eyes on the book I kept hidden under the desk. I had given up crying by now. You don't cry at school because of a name, do you? Anyhow, a person's true name, good or bad, is the one he earns for himself; and if people want to laugh – let them!

For all I've said about myself, one thing about me was pretty: my eyes. They were large and dark. Nearly everyone in Denmark has light blue eyes, so brown eyes are special. Oh, and another thing: I had dimples.

When I smiled, the grownups would say (grownups always feel they have to say something): "How cute! I wish I had dimples like that!" and they would pinch my cheek. And even though it hurt, I would go on smiling just to keep the dimples in place.

The family

I've already told you there were eight of us children. My parents used to divide us up into the four-big-ones and the four-little-ones. "Come, four-little-ones!" they would call, and we'd come running: Annette and Leonora, my sisters aged eight and nine, and my cousin Danny and me, both seven.

Leonora – or Leo

Leonora – known to us as Leo – was strong. Actually, she kept wishing she were a boy. Except on the Sabbath and holidays, she always wore boy's clothes, and at school played only with boys. And she, of all people, did have curls – long ones, dancing round her face and all over her forehead. It was thanks to her curls that we all thought she was very beautiful.

Being the eldest of us four-little-ones, Leo would decide what we were going to play. It took a lot of nerve to defy her. If I tried it all the same, she would declare right away: "Today I'm not playing and not speaking with Maya." And she wouldn't. She loved high jumping, running races, playing football, and riding a bicycle no-hands. I preferred staging plays about kings and queens and witches on our lawn, or putting on puppet shows. But when I asked Leo to join in, she'd say: "I'm fed up with your silly games. They're so dumb! Let's play football."

And that's how Leo remained the boss of the four-little-ones.

Annette

Annette was tall and pretty, and had green eyes. She was fond of small children and animals, and they loved her back. She would make a pet of any animal she found wandering about in the village. She had birds, fishes, turtles, cats and a dog; and she couldn't pass a baby without picking it up and cuddling it.

Danny

Danny was the naughtiest of us all. He did things like cutting up his shoes with a knife, drinking ink or writing on the walls. In short: You name it, Danny would do it. He and I were in the same class at school. Each morning when we entered the classroom, the teacher would greet us with: "You, Danny, come and sit here up front, or we won't have a moment's peace today." We didn't think that was fair.

My two brothers, Nissim and Koby

Now for the four-big-ones. Nissim and Koby, aged sixteen and thirteen, were like cat and dog. Not a minute passed without those two fighting over something. Nissim was a doer rather than a thinker, and was always out hunting. He would catch snails, rabbits, turtles, hedgehogs or anything else that came his way, and keep them in the wooden shed in our garden. With his fine clothes and long hair, he was friends with all the village girls. He hated school. Every once in a while he would run away from home, and I'd be sure he had gone to live with the Red Indians in America, or the Eskimos in Greenland. He always turned up again in the morning, though. I guess he never ran much further away than our garden shed.

Koby was the exact opposite. He was a good student and a great reader, and could sit for hours in his room, poring over his stamps and coins, playing his violin, or running his eyes dreamily over the lands and seas of the globe.

My older sisters, Bibi and Renate

Bibi and Renate were opposites, too, like a peacock and a safety pin. Bibi, who was fourteen, was big and womanly. She was full of laughter and jokes and songs, and if she wasn't cooking or baking or knitting, she was seated in front of a mirror. She could spend hours there, making up her face with white powder and red rouge, and trying on crazy hats – all for fun, because she never went to parties or dances.

Renate, twelve, was as serious as Bibi was merry. I never saw her laugh. Dressed in gray, looking grim in a pair of schoolmarmish glasses, she always had her nose stuck in a book. Renate didn't care about her looks and never did anything to make herself pretty. She even hated combing her hair. It was tough and frizzy, and any attempt to fix it would end in defeat and a couple of broken combs.

Mama, Papa and Miss Petersen

Our parents lived somewhere in another world. What contact we had with them was mainly through a go-between – Miss Petersen, our nanny. She had been living with us for fifteen years, and though she wasn't Jewish, she knew all the Jewish prayers, and all the dos and don'ts, as well as we did. She was tall and skinny, and had never married.

Papa was the master at home. We saw him only at suppertime, when we often sat for two hours at the table, listening to his stories about all the fantastic things that were going on in the world. He took the train every morning to Copenhagen, the Danish capital, where he worked in a government office. Mama was prettier than any of her daughters. She was fair and slender and had a kind face. Her head was always covered by the wig that religious Jewish women wear when they are married. She was forever busy about the house, because even with the help of Miss Petersen and Bente, the cook, there was plenty of work left taking care of a husband, eight children, a house and a garden.

Grandmother

Granny was short, fat and jolly. Her head, too, was always covered by a large wig. The rest of her was covered by long gray or black silk dresses, with a white collar for decoration. She was a widow. She didn't know any Danish, because she had come to Denmark from Germany when she was quite old already, and it's hard to learn a new language when you're old.

She had an apartment of her own in town, but in summertime she would come and stay with us, and then she would bake us cakes – cheesecakes and sweet crumbly ones. I used to sit and watch her making white cheese. We would sit in the garden, the sun high in the sky, clouds drifting over our heads like white sails on a blue ocean. Bees hummed and butterflies fluttered, the wild clover vied with our roses for beauty and fragrance, and the watery part of the sour milk filtered slowly through the thin muslin like a trickle of sand through an egg timer, leaving cheese on top. I would stick flowers through the mesh of a white chair, making a pattern, and it was as though time stood still.

They would seem to go on forever, those long days of summer, way up in the far north.

The house

Our house stood at the edge of a small village, where we were the only Jewish family. The house was really a mansion that had once belonged to a count, who had lived there with his family. He was a cousin of the Danish King, and the whole village had been his. Then he lost his money, sold the village, and kept only the house and garden for himself. In the end, he had to sell those, too, and my father bought them. It was a big house with three stories, an attic and a cellar.

The attic

The way to the attic was up a ladder and through a small trapdoor, but we only used to go there when we needed costumes for the Purim festival, or when the chimney sweep came.

The chimney sweep's visit was an event. It took place once a year, when the chimney needed cleaning, because we used wood or coal to heat the house, and all the smoke from our stoves went up the chimney.

He would arrive on his bicycle, all of him black, from the top of his top hat to the tips of his boots, his face included. He'd come armed with a long brush, a rope and a ladder, and we would all troop after him up to the attic.

How nice and warm it was up there! The sun would shine in through the tiny windows, its light like honey or beeswax, and the dust strung along its rays like pearls on a chain. On one side stood the dressing-up trunk full of clothes in every color, and the whole place smelled of the swallows that lived there.

We wouldn't come down until the chimney sweep had finished his job, picked up his ladder and gone off on his bicycle, and then we'd begin looking forward to his next visit.

The cellar

As nice as the attic was, so the cellar was scary. It was a creepy place: big and cold and damp and dark. On top of that, it was always crawling with mice, snakes and bats, while the walls were alive with mosquitoes.

Whenever Mama asked me to bring up potatoes from the cellar (we kept fruit and vegetables from our kitchen garden there), I would start shaking with fear. Going down the narrow staircase, I would whisper the Psalm of David: "Even though I walk through the valley of the shadow of death, I will fear no evil." I would repeat it over and over, and never stop until I got safely back up to the warm kitchen.

The garden

I'll describe the garden to you, because I lived there more than I lived in the house.

From the village, a lane ran between two rows of tall chestnut trees, ending in a big, strong gate. Once you had passed through this entrance, you felt you were inside a fairy tale.

In front of the house was an empty plot where the horses and carriages once stood. We four-little-ones used this as a sports field and a circus, or in other words, a stage for Leo's games.

In spring, when the snow was melting, our plot would be crisscrossed by rivers and brooks, and we would make plank-and-ladder-bridges to get about.

Beyond our plot was a huge lawn, full of small wild flowers, hedged by hazelnut bushes. At the far end was a large rhododendron shrub, which was our cave. We had made a nest of dry grass in its branches, and would crawl in there with books and games and food. We felt sure we were in China, because the rhododendron leaves were long and pointed like the fingernails of Chinese ladies.

But best of all was that no one knew that we were there. If called by Miss Petersen, we would wait a bit before coming out. An hour was like a full day to us, and a day like a year. So every additional minute was counted as pure gain.

Behind the house

Behind the house was a large field of grass, with a path on each side. A stone lion guarded each of the paths. During the winter we would slide on the snow there, and in the summer just roll on the grass. A big, sturdy, copper beech with red leaves grew in the middle of it. It wasn't just any tree, but a ship to sail in to faraway countries: to China and India, and sometimes to Greenland. The place wasn't safe though, because Miss Petersen could climb trees. It seemed as if nowhere in the world was safe, not even our big red tree – except, of course, our cave.

The grove

To the right of the lawn was a little grove. In there was where Adam and Eve had gone to hide after eating the apple. Many times when passing there, I thought I heard whisperings. Once I even made out Adam's voice saying: "Here I am," and sounding ashamed of himself. I had a feeling I'd seen Eve as well, all covered in long wavy hair and wearing a fig leaf. I think I heard her voice, but couldn't make out whether she was laughing or crying. At the end of the little grove was a gate leading to the other part of the village, but the truth is I never dared go as far as that. What would I have done if I'd really found two angels with flaming swords guarding the gate?

The nightingale

Now let's take the path to the left of the lawn. This led to the wooden shed where Nissim kept his rabbits and the rest of his animals. Behind it was a shrubbery, and in its depths a little nightingale lived and sang. I always imagined it was the same nightingale that had sung for the Emperor of China. Not that I ever saw it, but I spent hours listening to its song. And so, perhaps, did the cuckoo, which sometimes answered it like a distant echo.

Beyond the shrubbery was our kitchen garden, and then came the forest, a dark forest full of hollows and hiding places. I never went there alone, because I could never be sure I wouldn't meet the Big Bad Wolf, or Ali Baba and the Forty Thieves. (Maybe I also read too many stories.)

My world ended with the forest. I could wander all over the garden as much as I wished, but I wasn't allowed out of it on my own.

School

School was about an hour's walk from home. Every morning on our way there, we first had to pass a small lake, cross a wood, run quickly past houses with dogs barking at us, then walk for a bit along the railroad track, then pass a row of stores, a good-smelling bakery, a cobbler – and we were there.

The janitor would always shut the school gate right when the bell rang, and woe to the poor latecomer who was left outside.

And we – meaning Annette, Danny and I (never Leo) – were always late. Not on purpose, of course. It just happened. During the winter, it was having to get up in the dark and walk all that way through the snow; in the spring, it was the puddles that slowed us down. It would have been one thing if only we were punished – but the whole class was. Every Saturday, our teacher would tell one chapter from a story with lots of suspense. She only told it, though, if none of the kids in class had been late even once all week. We ourselves didn't care if she told it or not. We didn't go to school on Saturday anyway, Saturday being our Sabbath. It was wrong of us, of course. We should have thought of all the other kids. But we were little and we didn't.

One day, being late for school again, we saw a British paratrooper land in a tree in the field. We started running, but he was gone when we got to the tree, and we only found the kids from our school standing around it, looking at the white parachute that had settled on the branches like some huge, fantastic bird, foreshadowing things to come.

The neighbors

Our nearest neighbors were cows. They always stood on the other side of our gate, munching grass all day and every day, come rain, come shine.

To the right of our garden lived an orchestra conductor. I never saw him, but I liked to listen to the beautiful music coming from his house. From the back gate at the bottom of our garden, a path led to the village. Beyond this path came a wood. Beyond the wood came the sea, and beyond the sea, lay Sweden.

To the left of the garden lived a family that was different from everyone else. I have told you that our house had once belonged to a count who owned the whole village. Well, there was another village, not far from ours, and that one had belonged to another count. He had lived next door to us, but his house and garden were far bigger. When he decided to sell his house, it was bought by a rich Arab sheikh. The sheikh had married a Danish woman, but they lived in the Arab style even so.

They had two sons, and while we walked our long morning road to school on foot, they would be driving in a carriage drawn by two white horses, with a uniformed coachman sitting on top. He held a long whip in his hand, that coachman. When he reached our school, he would leap from his seat and open the carriage door. Out came the two boys, dressed in black, their heads covered by a red tasseled fez.

Today you may see Arab men wearing a fez like that almost anywhere in the world, but in a small village in Denmark in those days, no one ever had. The two boys did not speak to us. I think they spoke to no one. Maybe it was on account of living in the grandest house in the village. Or maybe they just didn't speak to anyone.

And that's how, long ago, in an out-of-the-way northern village, a Jewish family and an Arab family lived peacefully together as neighbors, each in their own home, their own castle.

Fetching the milk

We were a religious family. We didn't even buy our milk from the milkman, for fear it might have got a drop of milk from a pig or some other forbidden animal in it. Instead, we would go to fetch it at a farm every day – an hour-and-a-half's walk through the fields. The first person we always met on arrival was a big, wild-looking boy who was deaf and dumb, and was always sitting on a swing staring at us. We would stare back at him, and never knew whether he didn't find us just as peculiar as we found him.

We would take our bucket to the cowshed, fill it with fresh milk, and start back for home through fields of clover and buzzing bees. And more than once the milk turned sour on the way, what with having been shaken up and churned for an hour-and-a-half.

The Sabbath

The Sabbath day meant prayers, good things to eat, clean clothes and the Bible.

The whole family stayed at home on the Sabbath, and after breakfast we would read the weekly portion of the Bible in Hebrew together, translating every sentence into Danish.

(I myself wouldn't wait for the translation, but would sneak a look at the Danish text printed beside the Hebrew.)

When we read of the Land of Israel there, I thought of it as a kind of dreamland. A land flowing with milk and honey? I didn't understand how such a thing could be. A land of grapes and olives, of figs and pomegranates? I had never seen those fruits in my life.

Our connection with the Jewish people was through the biblical heroes of long ago, and we felt closer to Abraham, Moses and King David than to the living Jews of our own time. We knew we belonged to the Jewish people, but we had little contact with any of them wherever they lived in the world – till our world fell apart.

PART TWO
THE RESCUE

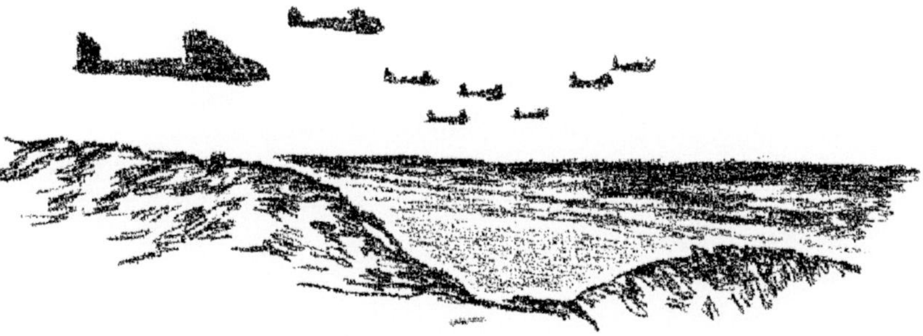

The first planes

One day I was standing in the bedroom with Mama, when all of a sudden there came a great roaring noise. We went out on the balcony – and for the first time in my life, I saw airplanes in the sky. They flew right over our house, and then on, over the wood, to the sea on the horizon. It was April 9, 1940 – the day Germany invaded Denmark.

Denmark outmatched

Denmark is a small country, about one-third the size of New York State. It follows that it only had a small army and very few weapons. Germany, on the other hand, was large and powerful. The Germans had spent years getting ready for war. They dreamed of conquering the whole world and becoming its rulers. What could a tiny country like Denmark do against such a mighty power? What's more, Denmark had never prepared for war, wanting to remain neutral and not have to fight at all.

Early that morning, when their army crossed the border, the Germans promised the Danish government that if they did not resist, they would allow Denmark to maintain its independence and run its own affairs. The King and the government protested the German aggression and the breach of Denmark's neutrality. Yet they decided to accept the German offer and not to fight, in order to spare the people much suffering. Denmark was occupied by the Germans in a single day.

The occupation

Unlike all the other people of Europe conquered by Germany, the Danes were left more or less unharmed for three full years. The Germans hardly interfered with their day-to-day life. Denmark pretended it was still neutral and the Germans accepted this pretense, that is, as long as it suited their interests.

The Danish government was allowed to run the country during these years. Still, there were plenty of German soldiers about. They seemed to feel quite at home in Denmark, and looked as if they were enjoying their stay.

The Jews of Denmark were left in peace. In all the rest of occupied Europe, they were driven out of their homes, shut up in ghettos and from there sent to concentration camps. The Germans constantly demanded that the government pass special laws against the Jews in the country, but the government rejected every such demand. Thus, the Danish Jews could live where they liked, go where they wished, and work anywhere they chose. They were not even made to wear the yellow Star of David on their chests, though that was about the first thing the Germans forced the Jews to do in any other country they occupied.

The King and the Yellow Star

The King of Denmark, King Christian the Tenth, was already quite an old man at that time. He used to ride his horse through the streets of Copenhagen every day. He did not give up that habit even after the German conquest, but would appear faithfully on his horse each morning to greet his people. He was a symbol of national pride and independence to them.

When the King heard that the Germans had demanded that the Jews of Denmark wear the Yellow Star, he declared that in that case everyone would wear a Yellow Star; so the Germans dropped the matter.

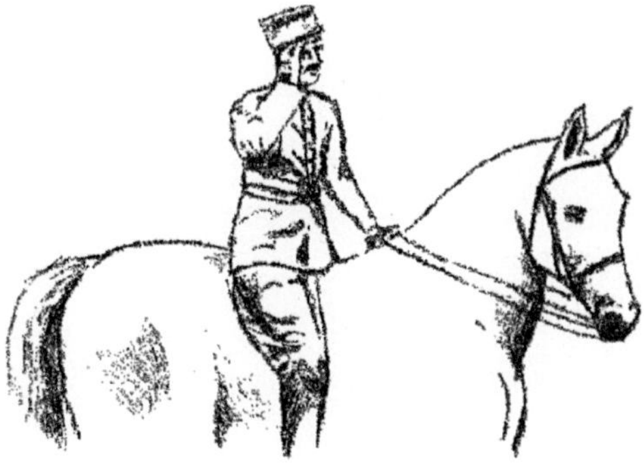

The change

So for three years, we, along with all the other people of Denmark, lived more or less as we always had. Then, in the late summer of 1943, the Germans changed their policy.

Following strikes and acts of sabotage by Danish resistance fighters, the Germans decided to treat Denmark like every other country they had occupied. The Danish government resigned and the Germans declared a state of emergency. The King was placed under house arrest in one of his castles.

Ships were sent from Germany to pick up the Danish Jews – all 7,000 of them – and take them away to concentration camps. Secret orders went out to arrest all the Jews on the night of October 1. That was the night of Rosh Hashanah, the Jewish New Year, and the Germans assumed that on such an important holiday, the Jews would all be at home.

First warning

Georg Duckwitz was a German living in Denmark, who worked as shipping agent at the German Embassy in Copenhagen. He heard about the secret plan from the German Governor of Denmark, who now ruled the country, and went to tell the head of the Danish Labor Party. This man, in turn, immediately called in the leader of the Jewish community and informed him of the German plan. The Jewish leader would not believe him. "You are lying to me!" he cried, and it took a long time before he was convinced. (The same thing happened over and over in other countries as well. The Jews simply could not believe that the fearful tales about ghettos and concentration camps were true.)

That same day, the Jewish community leader went to Rabbi Marcus Melchior, the Chief Rabbi's deputy, and told him what he had heard. (The Chief Rabbi himself had been arrested about a month earlier, along with other leaders of the Jewish community.)

The Rabbi's announcement

The next day was the day before Rosh Hashanah. Early that morning, before prayers in the great synagogue of Copenhagen, Rabbi Melchior told the people in the synagogue of the German plan. He instructed them to leave their homes at once, and not come to the synagogue on the holy day. He also urged them to pass his message on to all the other Jews in Denmark.

And they did. All that day, the message was passed on from one to the other, till it had reached almost all the members of the community. No one said: "You must leave home because the Germans are coming to arrest you." Instead, they used a sort of secret code, such as: "Come and visit Aunt Hanne at once!" or "Grandma is ill. Go to see her now!" or "It's Tove's birthday. She needs your help urgently!"

Leaving

No one came to the synagogue the next morning. Nearly all the Jews left their homes and moved in with non-Jewish friends, or hid in hospitals or churches.

Only a few people were caught by the Germans, either because the message had not reached them, or because they did not escape in time, or because they refused to believe the danger was real. Our Granny was one of them. She stayed at her home in Copenhagen, and the Germans came for her and sent her to a concentration camp.

But she was the exception. When the Germans reached the Jewish homes on Rosh Hashanah night as planned, they found most of them empty. Out of Copenhagen's 6,000 Jews, less than 300 were caught, mostly old people who had not managed to get away.

The underground

The Danish underground resistance movement was by then fighting a secret war against the German occupiers. Its members did what they could to make trouble for the Germans, and carried out different acts of sabotage. They now came to the aid of the

Jews, looking for ways to help them escape from their homes and save them from being caught. They arranged for them to get to the coast, and from there, in fishing boats across the sea to the safety of Sweden, which was neutral and not taking part in the war. The Swedish government had just announced publicly that refugees from Denmark could come and stay in Sweden.

At the same time, the Bishop of Copenhagen, who was head of the Danish Church, published a declaration, saying: "It is our duty to help our Jewish brothers and sisters in this time of danger." This was read out by the priests in all the churches in Denmark.

The fishermen

There are many small villages along the Danish coast, and most of the men living there are fishermen. Each village has a small fishing harbor of its own.

When asked by the underground to help get the Jews to Sweden, nearly all the fishermen agreed, though they knew it meant risking their own lives. With great courage and skill, they carried out the difficult operation of moving thousands of people across the sea in a very short time. (Those who could, paid the fishermen for rescuing them.)

That is how most of Denmark's Jews were saved – more than six thousand who lived in the capital city, Copenhagen, and another thousand who were scattered in farms and villages throughout the country. Most of these were young refugees who had escaped from Germany just before the war. In Denmark, they were learning to be farmers, preparing themselves for a new life in *Eretz Israel* (the Land of Israel).

Our Rosh Hashanah dinner

While the Jews of Copenhagen were preparing to escape, we were preparing to celebrate Rosh Hashanah. We had heard nothing and we knew nothing about the roundup. We were sitting at the dinner table on Rosh Hashanah day, when we heard someone knocking at the door. It was Tito Wessel, a friend of my father from the Foreign Office.

"What are you doing here?" he cried. "Don't you know that all the Jews of Copenhagen have already left their homes and gone into hiding?" No, we didn't.

"Haven't you heard of the big ship waiting in the harbor of Copenhagen to take away all the Jews of Denmark? You must get out of the house at once! Now!"

He went, leaving a shocked silence behind. What should we do? Where could we go? A big family like ours – eight children, two parents, a nanny and a cook. And on Rosh Hashanah, too!

Should we go or stay?

More knocks. Nobody moved. My father's friend again. "Go!" he urged us. "At once! At once!"

A white sheet

My parents decided we should leave the house and move in with neighbors for the night. Only Miss Petersen would stay behind. If the Germans did not come, she would hang a white sheet from the window. If they did – no sheet.

The next morning, we approached the house cautiously – and there was the white sheet. We went in and began making preparations for departure. Where to, though?

We packed some clothes and other necessities, and ordered two taxis. We would move to another village, my parents decided, and then wait and see what happened.

Having packed, we straightened up the house to leave it nice and clean. Who for? What for? My mother made sandwiches for the journey. I think Mama still didn't quite believe that what we had been told was true. I think she believed we would come back in a day or so.

In the taxi

And then we were driving past fields and woods, and I whispered to myself: "Goodbye house. Goodbye garden. Goodbye school. Goodbye village. Where are we going?"

Koby said: "We shouldn't have left at all. We'll be back tomorrow. People just got the jitters. Nothing's going to happen, you'll see."

I said nothing. What did I know?

At the hotel

At last, we reached a village called Hillerød, which was farther away from the coast than ours. We entered the hotel. Most villages in Denmark have a main square, where there is a small hotel or inn. So here we were, a family with eight children turning up in the middle of the day and asking for rooms. How could we fail to attract attention?

The hotel was full of German soldiers. They were sitting in the restaurant downstairs, eating and drinking beer. Had they seen us? We hurried up to our rooms on the top floor, where we would stay for the night. That night was very dark, and there were mice in our rooms, too, but we had to stay until we knew where to go. The night passed. Thank God, nothing happened.

In the morning, Mama and Miss Petersen went out to buy a newspaper, and find out what was happening. On the front page of the paper, it said: "The Germans have taken away all the Danish Jews. Denmark has no more Jews." Only then did we realize that my father's friend had been right. We thought that of all the Jews of Denmark, we alone were left.

To the farm

We remained in our hotel rooms until nightfall. The family of Bente, our cook, had a farm in the neighborhood, and that's where we decided to go. We went that evening in a cart, drawn by two strong horses, and piled high with straw. We children were under the straw, hidden from sight. We arrived at the farm, and made quickly for the kitchen in the back. I still remember that kitchen. Not the way it looked, so much as the way it smelt all over of smoked cheese.

Would we stay here?

No. Bente's family was afraid to let us stay, but invited us in for dinner. Then we left Bente with her family and drove on through the night, just going on, with no idea where to. All at once, Miss Petersen remembered she knew of a lady, a Miss Jansen, who had a small castle somewhere near. Maybe she would agree to hide us? We thought we'd try her. What else could we do? And this time we were lucky: She received us with open arms to her home, Havreholm Castle.

The search for us

Now that at least for a little while we were safe, I'll tell you what happened after we left home on Rosh Hashanah. Only a few hours later, German soldiers arrived with a big truck to take us away. It was dark outside, because in Denmark, as in all the northern countries, night comes early in the fall and winter: at four in the afternoon, it is pitch dark already. (In summertime, it's just the other way around: In midsummer there's still daylight at eleven o'clock at night!) The Germans surrounded the garden, blocking both the main gate and the two back gates. Then they went in. They had brought police dogs and big flashlights. They banged on the door, but no one opened, so they shined their flashlights through the windows to see if we were hiding in there.

Then they searched the garden. They went all over it with their flashlights, and turned the dogs loose, to help hunt for us. Then, finding no one, they left. They did not break down the doors or smash the windows. They did not rob the house, or burn it down. They did all these things, and worse, in the other countries of Europe. But Denmark was different. And so they just left as they had come, in the truck that was meant to take us to the waiting ship. Left, and went on to search other Jewish homes on their list.

The underground on our tracks

Another group of people had come to look for us, soon after the Germans. They, too, did not find us, but decided to go on looking. These were the underground resistance fighters I told you about. They had come to take us to a safe hiding place near the sea.

They managed to trace us as far as the farm, but there they lost our trail and turned back. Yet all that time we were so near, only half an hour's drive from the farm, and unaware of either the Germans or the underground looking for us. So, while most of the Jews of Denmark were already escaping across the sea, or had even reached Sweden already, we just sat there in our castle and did nothing.

Our fellow refugees

There were two other people hiding from the Germans in the castle. One was a pianist, who had never known he was a Jew, until the Germans found out that one of his grandfathers had been Jewish. For the Germans, that was enough to make him a Jew as well.

He used to sit at the piano all day, and far into the night, playing and playing. Most of all he played Chopin, and his music would fill the house. The other refugee was a hospital nurse called Kirsten. She wasn't Jewish, but she was the girlfriend of an underground member who had escaped to Sweden, and she wanted to join him. She was always laughing, as though she didn't have a care in the world. She seemed, in fact, to treat it all as an exciting adventure. Come to think of it, she had nothing to be afraid of, really. Even if the Germans had caught her, they would have let her go again because she wasn't Jewish. I didn't know yet that being far away from your boyfriend can also hurt a lot.

The bewitched castle

Actually, I wasn't much afraid myself. I didn't understand what was happening, or what might yet happen to us. I knew, of course, that we were fleeing from the Germans and that if caught we would be sent to the camps, but I didn't worry. I felt sure we had come to Sleeping Beauty's castle at last, and could sleep here for a hundred years. I would have liked nothing better. The castle was so beautiful. It was just like a fairy-tale place. It had a magnificent park, and in the middle of it, a lake with boats. Most wonderful of all, it had an attic, and in the attic a small, snug room full of children's books. And that's where I spent my days, reading about princes and princesses, good kings and wicked lords. I felt as if the whole world around me was asleep, and even the sound of Chopin's music could not wake it. And so the time passed, and every day was like a year. We waited and waited. The world was on fire – and we did nothing.

Plans

My father soon grew restless. He couldn't just sit and wait any longer. My parents spent hours talking to the lady of the castle, and what she told them only made them more anxious. Now they learned what the Germans had been planning for the Jews, and they understood that our only hope lay in escape to Sweden. We would have to find a fisherman willing to take the risk. Then we would have to find a way to get to the coast. How? When? We didn't know yet.

One evening, Papa was looking more cheerful. Miss Jansen had found a fisherman, and Papa had already talked to him. I heard him tell Mama: "The fisherman is ready. He has a boat. Now we have to wait for calm seas so we can cross safely."

More waiting. The pianist had already left. He had found a place in another boat. The nurse Kirsten, it was decided, would go with us.

Waiting, waiting. My father was getting nervous again. We wouldn't be able to stay here much longer for the Germans might yet find us in the end. We had to get away fast.

At last, the day came. We said goodbye to Miss Petersen, and prepared to go.

The way to the fishing village

The plan was for each of us to get to the fishing harbor on his own. That way we would attract less attention. We could not carry a suitcase or bag, or anything else that would show we were going on a journey. But our greatest problem was that the way to the fishing village went right past Horserod, a German army camp.

Each of us children was given a bicycle. I got the smallest, because I was the smallest, only just seven. (But to ride a bicycle – that I already knew when I was four. All the kids in Denmark can ride a bicycle almost before they can walk.) My parents came in a taxi.

We put on as many clothes as possible. That way, we could at least take something with us. I was wearing two dresses, two sweaters, a coat, three pairs of socks, a hat, a scarf, mittens and sturdy boots. It's a good thing it was fall and starting to get cold, otherwise we would have looked even more peculiar, dressed in all those layers like an Egyptian mummy. And it wasn't just peculiar, it was awfully uncomfortable, too.

We set out early in the morning. Slowly, one by one, we rode our bicycles toward the sea. Imagine that ride – in bulky clothes, hardly able to move an arm, and all the time thinking of the camp with all its German soldiers ahead!

We made it. One by one we reached the small harbor of Hornbaek – and were together again.

At the harbor

It was a sleepy fall day, cold and damp. Heavy clouds hung low overhead. Seagulls swooped over the gray-green waves, shrieking. The fishing boats had gone out to sea already. Only one was left in the harbor, its fisherman busy with his nets. He was in no hurry at all. Now and then he carried some tools to his boat, checked the motor, taking his time about it.

There were few people around, only some old fishermen, sitting on a bench, saying how cold it was, recalling past adventures, basking in the glow of their memories.

As in every Danish fishing harbor, there was a pub; this one was just where the jetty started. In the pub, and in front of it, German soldiers were sitting, drinking beer, laughing and carefree as though the whole world belonged to them.

And we – how could we fail to arouse suspicion? Eight children moving clumsily in layers of clothing, when all the other children were at school now, so what were we doing here anyway? How would we ever get past those frightening Germans? It seemed impossible.

Yet it looks as if sometimes even the impossible happens. How else can I explain that we did manage to slip past the pub one by one, reach the boat and crawl below decks.

Sometimes I think that maybe the soldiers were so full of themselves and their beer that they didn't see us. Or maybe somebody paid them to look the other way. And sometimes I think that they just didn't want to see us.

In the boat

Koby was lucky. He got to stay on deck with the fisherman. I wasn't allowed to go up there, because I was little, and had to stay down below in the hold with the grownups. I was longing to be out in the sea air, not sit in the dark and breathe the stink of fish.

And still the fisherman didn't sail. He was waiting for noon, when there would be few people about. At last, he took the helm, and at that moment the head of a Danish policeman appeared above us. He was standing on the jetty and looking down at our boat in the water. Was all lost? Had we been discovered? No. The policeman gave a broad smile, saluted smartly and called: "Have a good trip!" Then he turned and was gone.

That's how we knew that the Danish police were not working together with the Germans.

And in this, too, Denmark was different from most other occupied countries.

On the high seas

We were on our way. The sea was stormy, the waves high, and the boat rose and fell. Kirsten, usually so cheerful, went strangely quiet. Then her face turned green, and she was sick. Next, it was Leo's turn.

We were approaching the mid-sea borderline between Denmark and Sweden. German gunboats were patrolling the border here, and we had to wait for darkness to slip across. Our fisherman, therefore, began sailing the boat up and down, this way and that, pulling his nets through the water, pretending to be busy catching fish, not smuggling people.

The crossing

I've already told you that in the countries of the north, it gets dark around four o'clock in the fall. It was a good thing for us, because as soon as it got dark, the fisherman gathered his nets, started the motor and set off for the border. We were all crowded in the hold, and the awful reek of fish and vomit got stronger and stronger.

"I'll die if I don't go up for a minute," I thought, and asked Mama if I could. Mama was busy with Leo and Kirsten though, and took no notice of me. I decided not to wait for an answer but go on deck anyhow. Even halfway up the steps I already felt the touch of cool clean air on my face. I took a deep breath and tasted the sea salt on my lips.

Koby was steering the boat. He was at the helm and the fisherman was teaching him how to use the map and compass.

"Good you came up." The fisherman smiled at me. "How are the others down there?"

"Um," I said, "a bit seasick."

"We'll soon reach the border," he said, "and the weather is improving, too."

I was just thinking I had better go back below, when the fisherman asked if I'd like to help Koby steer. Did I!

We sailed on. Koby and me at the helm. All was quiet. The fisherman took a pipe from his pocket and began to smoke, his eyes searching the water. All at once, he stiffened. He craned his neck, and growled: "Bloody Germans!" We saw a pinpoint of light in the distance, growing bigger and bigger as it approached us. A German gunboat was coming our way.

"Hold on to the helm," the fisherman told Koby softly. He put out his pipe and hurriedly cut the motor. Then he picked up a large net and cast it into the water. The German boat was coming nearer. When they passed us, the Germans saw a peaceful fisherman, completely taken up with his work, and not even sparing the time to glance at them. They suspected nothing and continued on their way.

Koby heaved a great sigh and wiped the sweat from his forehead. But the fisherman went on calmly with his "work" for another half hour. Only then did he pull in his net, start the motor again, and point the boat in the direction of the border – and Sweden. Suddenly the fisherman noticed me. "What are you doing there?" he asked. I had been so scared that I had hidden in a dark corner of the boat, and hadn't dared get up till now. "Come on," he said, "it's your turn at the helm. Koby and I must take care of the net and remove the fish we've caught."

The sea had calmed down. The sky, too, had cleared, and showed thousands of twinkling stars. Maybe they wished to light our way safely to the border. Now we had almost reached it, and the fisherman took over the helm.

"There are lots of underwater mines here," Koby whispered to me. We both stared hard at the water to see if it looked all right, or if perhaps we would suddenly spot one. But our fisherman knew the way well. It wasn't the first time he had sailed it. He steered the boat firmly and steadily out of the danger zone, and into the territorial waters of Sweden.

We had crossed the border! The danger was past. Everyone came up on deck and sighed with relief. A tremendous weight was lifted off our shoulders, and with it came a great sense of peace.

Then we saw lights in the distance. It had been three years since we had seen lights at night, because a blackout was in force throughout Denmark. And here lights were shining at us in a merry greeting.

A ship with a Swedish flag, blue and yellow, was coming to meet us. Smiling sailors called out: "Welcome to Sweden!"

I have never heard more beautiful words.

We now had to leave our fishing boat, which had to return to Denmark, and climb aboard the much bigger Swedish navy ship that would bring us to harbor. Somehow, with the help of the Swedish sailors, we managed!

In harbor

And there, like in a dream or a fairy tale, there in the harbor of Helsingborg, people whom we knew from Copenhagen were waving at us. How come? Hadn't we read in the paper that all the Jews of Denmark had been taken away by the Germans?

We landed. And as Mama was hugging and kissing the people who were welcoming us, we learned that most of Denmark's Jews had managed to escape to Sweden, and that we ourselves were among the last. Only Grandmother, our dear sweet Granny, had not arrived. It was the night before Yom Kippur, the Day of Atonement – a day of fasting and prayer, and the last of the Ten Days of Awe starting with Rosh Hashanah. We had left home on Rosh Hashanah, and reached Sweden on Yom Kippur eve, after our own days of awe.

Questions

There was one question I never asked in all those days: Why us? Why the Jews? What had we done? I simply accepted the fact that there were evil people in the world, like the Germans who wanted to kill, and good ones, like the underground people and the fishermen who wanted to save others even at risk to their own lives.

It was only much later that I learnt about the Holocaust, in which six million Jews were murdered, and how of all the countries occupied by the Germans, only Denmark refused to let its Jews be taken away and killed.

And so at least one Jewish community was saved.

You may ask: What is one small community of six or seven thousand people, compared with six million? I can only answer with the ancient Jewish saying: "To save one life is like saving a whole world."

PART THREE
FOREST HAVEN

Sweden

Sweden is a large country with a small population. It is a country of forests, of mountains and lakes, and of peace. Sweden has not been at war for over one hundred years. It is a kingdom, and its kings often live to be a hundred. At the time we arrived, the Swedish King was only ninety. He spent most of his days in a rocking chair. His hobby was embroidering pretty tablecloths and cushions, and sometimes he played tennis to keep fit.

He and his government offered us refuge. I guess they didn't believe that a few thousand Jewish refugees would disturb Sweden's peace.

In the refugee camp

For the first few days, we stayed at a temporary refugee camp at Ramlösa, not far from the port of Helsingborg. We met many other Danish Jews there, along with some Danish policemen. They, too, had been forced to flee from the Germans, and had been smuggled over in the same fishing boats. After a while, most of the refugees moved to the small towns and villages in the neighborhood, from where they could always see the coast of Denmark on the horizon.

Stockholm

We ourselves moved farther north, going by train to Stockholm, the capital of Sweden. There we were met at the station by people from the Jewish community. They had found us two rooms to live in for the first weeks, in an apartment next to a small synagogue. Once we had settled in, they came to visit us, stare at us, ask questions and give advice.

Mrs. Bluestone

One of our visitors was a rich old woman. At least, I thought she was rich, because she wore a glittery ring with a blue stone on each finger, and the fur of a fat red fox round her neck. Her hair was red, too – dyed red, and made up in curls that sprang out from under a black hat. Her face was covered by a thin black veil. Through it you could see a pair of thick lips painted red as red, wrinkled cheeks with white powder on them, and a nose with a big shiny wart. What a face!

At first, I was sure she had fallen in love with Papa, because she wouldn't let him be. She would come, sit next to him, talk and talk and smile at him. When she smiled, she smacked her lips. She smelt of perfume all over, and she always brought us candy.

Before long it turned out it wasn't Papa she had fallen in love with, but me. She had no husband or children, and she was nearly seventy, and fancied she would like a little girl of her own.

And so it happened that one morning I said goodbye to my family, and went with Mrs. Bluestone to her house downtown. It was freezing outside, and an icy wind bit into my face. I was on the verge of tears, and kept choking them back, unable to swallow, unable to talk. And Mrs. Bluestone just kept smiling at me and smacking her lips. My eyes hurt. Now and then, a tear brimmed over, turning into an ice drop halfway down my cheek. My hands and feet had frozen, too, and I could barely move them.

At last, we reached Mrs. Bluestone's apartment in the center of Stockholm. It was dark and warm inside. All the windows had large, heavy curtains that kept out the light. The apartment was filled with rugs, sofas, armchairs and small tables. Every table had an embroidered tablecloth on it, and in the middle a plate with cookies or candy. Little glass and china figurines of animals and people stood all over the place.

Mrs. Bluestone was very excited to have me. She had bought me a big doll and a new dress. She rushed back and forth through the house, and when she no longer knew what to do with herself, she went shopping. I sat in an armchair in the dark living room and looked at the little china figures.

I think that's what I did for the next few days, too, just sat and stared and felt miserable.

Maybe I could open a curtain, though, and at least see the sky? A little swallow stood on the windowsill, a cute little china swallow, smooth to the touch – like the swallows in our attic at home. If I took it in my hand and kissed it and wished very hard, maybe it would turn into a real swallow and we'd fly off together to...at that moment I heard footsteps in the hall and – smash! – the swallow dropped to the floor and broke its wings. What now? Find glue and mend it? No time. Find somewhere to hide it? No time either. Better return the poor bird to its place on the windowsill, close the curtain and...Leo! Leo stood before me.

"What's wrong with you?" she asked. "Why are you crying?"

"I don't know," I said. "I don't know why. The tears just keep coming all the time. And the time, too, just goes on and on," I sighed.

Leo laughed and took some cookies from the table. "Listen," she said, "we've moved to a new place in the suburbs. It's a small apartment on the ground floor." She paused to eat another cookie. "And the house is right next to a huge forest. You've never seen such a forest."

"Is it as big as ours?" I asked.

"A hundred times bigger. And it's got all these trees, you've never seen anything like it. And you can jump through our window and be right in the forest. It's yummy."

Leo stopped to think whether she had done right to tell me.

"Great," I said, beginning to choke on my tears again.

"And how's Mrs. Bluestone?" asked Leo to change the subject, and having finished off the cookies started on the candy. "Listen, Maya," she said putting on a mysterious face, "D'you know what's the most exciting thing about the forest?" She waited a moment, then said: "It's got a big monster troll living in it!"

"What does he look like?" I asked, shivering a little.

"Well, he's got red curly hair, and he's got a nose as long as a beanpole, with a wart on top, and his lower lip hangs down to his tummy, and he's got a long tail as well. I didn't actually see him myself." Leo giggled. "I guess he left the forest and is living in town and..." She paused, looked carefully all around the room, then lowered her voice to a whisper: "He eats little girls!"

I looked around the room, too, saw the curtain and began to shake.

"Right," said Leo, "I've got to go." The candy, too, was all gone by now. "I just came to town to buy schoolbooks." But before she could reach the door, there was Mama, together with Mrs. Bluestone.

"Time to come home," said Mama. "Thank Mrs. Bluestone nicely for having you."

I made a deep curtsy, taking a quick peep under Mrs. Bluestone's skirt to see if there really was a tail there.

"Now I can see your dimples at last," said Mrs. Bluestone, smacking her lips as she stroked my cheek. And then the ice melted inside me, and I burst into a great flood of tears, and didn't stop crying till we were out of town.

We go fishing

"It's bitter cold," said Mama. "Mind you dress warmly, all of you."

It was cold. We were in the middle of winter. Everything was covered with snow, and all the lakes had frozen over. The moment you went out, you felt your hands and feet just disappear on you, followed by your nose and ears.

And it was just such a cold day that Danny suggested: "Let's go fishing today after school. There are lots of boats by the lake in the forest. We can take one of them."

"Huh!" said Leo, practical as always. "You can't. The lake's all frozen. I went skating on it myself only yesterday."

"So what?" said Danny. "Today's sunny, and I bet some of the ice has melted already. We'll look for holes and fish in them." Leo stuck to her opinion, but Annette agreed right away. Annette always agreed to everything, while I always shilly-shallied. Still, what did I have to lose! If we didn't succeed, we could always simply go home.

We had become street kids in Sweden. We were on our own most of the day, because Mama had had to go out to work as well as Papa, to help provide for our large family.

And that's how after school that day, we went, Annette, Danny and I, to fish in the lake.

We didn't have a proper fishing rod, just a stick with a piece of string, and some hooks we had bought to tie to it. We found three boats by the lake. We pushed and pulled but couldn't move them, because they were full of snow and ice. They were like three white bears that refuse to wake up from their winter sleep.

"What'll we do?" asked Annette.

"Walk out over the ice till we find a hole, and then fish," said Danny.

The ice was slippery. Here and there it was quite thin, and you could see the water underneath, but we didn't find a hole. I volunteered to go on looking, while Annette and Danny returned to check the ice near the shore. I walked on, getting further and further away from them.

Suddenly I heard Annette calling: "Come back, come back!" She was waving her hands wildly. "Maya! You're crazy! Come here!" I made to turn back, but then I thought: Why not scare them a bit? Just look at them getting all jittery! "Maya!" they were shouting together now. "Come back quick! It's dangerous!"

But I walked on. I'd show them I was no scaredy-cat like them. And then all at once – cr-r-r-rack – the ice split under my feet and – splash! – I went down into the freezing water. I had found a hole all right!

"Help!" I screamed, and my head went under the water. Danny and Annette were already racing across the ice like mad, and it was a lucky thing the ice didn't crack under their running feet. Then they reached me, and fished me out.

"You dummy!" said Annette furiously. "You nearly drowned! And what'd we have told Papa and Mama then?"

"Let's run home fast," said Danny, "and maybe we'll get there before them." We started running as fast as we could – which was pretty slow: my coat was heavy with water, producing a long trail of puddles behind me. Thank goodness, we didn't meet anyone on the way home. There we waited outside, while Annette tiptoed quietly in to take stock of the situation. She came back like a spy with bad news: "Papa and Mama are home. We'll have to stay out till your clothes are dry."

And only after dark, and after it had started snowing and after I had turned into a block of ice, did we go inside at last.

"So?" Leo asked us mockingly. "How many fish did you catch?"

"Just one," said Annette proudly, "but a big one!"

And that was the end of our fishing adventure.

Waiting for spring

The Swedish winter is long and cold. For months, the sun never shows itself. It would still be dark when we went to school in the morning, and even during the few hours of daylight, you hardly ever got a glimpse of blue sky. Snowstorms, fog, clouds, icy winds and toward nightfall, wolves howling in the forest as they went on the hunt. Bad as winter might be, there was one thing that almost made up for it, and that was sledding. We had a cardboard box for a sleigh, and nothing was more fun than to sit in it and whoosh down the mountains of snow in the forest. Or maybe one thing was better still: when the winter ended at last, and it was spring.

A strange visitor

One evening a man called on us, and asked to speak to Papa "in absolute privacy." He was Jewish and his name was Mr. Adler. He had escaped from Germany to Denmark when the war broke out, and then from Denmark to Sweden in 1943 like the rest of us. He was short and skinny, and dressed all in black. His face was pale, but lit up by sparkling green eyes. His hair was black. A straight parting started at the forehead, dividing his hair into two equal halves.

Papa and Mr. Adler shut themselves up in the living room, and we kids stood behind the door and listened to their "absolutely private" conversation. Mr. Adler had thought up a plan to smuggle the King of Denmark into Sweden. Like many other people, he was worried about the King's fate under the German occupation. His idea was to dig a tunnel under the sea between Denmark and Sweden, and then take the King through. He had thought of everything: how to get the King from his palace to the seashore, how to dig the tunnel without hitting the underwater mines, and so on and so forth. The conversation lasted nearly all night.

I already had a picture in my mind of the King riding on his horse under the water, waving right and left to the surprised fishes, and them gazing at him openmouthed.

But of course nothing came of it all, as it was a crazy idea to start with, and the King stayed in Denmark throughout the war. It would have been nice, though.

A day in the forest

Leo had been right: The forest near our house was enormous. In summertime, it was full of wild blueberries, too. And if you have ever tasted blueberries, you will never forget their special bittersweet taste.

Leo and I had gone picking berries for all the family. Leo filled one basket after another, and when she could carry no more, went home. My baskets weren't full yet, so I stayed and went on picking. It was warm and pleasant in the forest, and I knew I had many hours left before the sun went down. I didn't see any bears, though I looked for them behind every tree; tall pine trees they were, looking like half-opened sunshades. A sweet smell came from the delicate white bells of the lilies of the valley, which peeped out from the green moss.

All at once, I heard a happy tune in the distance, seeming to come from another world. I set out through the forest.

"Where's it from?" I wondered, as I made my way toward the music, now and then stopping to eat berries, or to pick a lily for my dried-flower collection, or just to lie down for a rest on the soft moss. And close my eyes for a minute.

They came from all sides of the forest, the white lilies of the valley. They bowed to each other, nodded their heads and said over and over – maybe a hundred times: "Please," "Thank you," "Thank you,"

"Please" – because that's what people do in Sweden, and they wanted to show what very polite flowers they were. Then they danced and sang. Blueberries jumped down from their bushes and rolled on the ground laughing. Then they got up, whistled, and invited the lilies to dance. But the lilies pretended they were too shy. They were so busy being shy, that they even forgot to tinkle their bells.

When I woke up, it was nearly dark, which was bad enough, and I didn't know where I was, which was awful. Then I saw a light in the distance. The light belonged to a little hut, and all at once I realized that the music belonged to it, too. Thank goodness, I said to myself, and hurried toward it.

There were two people in the hut, and one of them was Bibi. The other was a tall young man, who was playing the flute for her.

"What are you doing here?" Bibi asked in surprise when she saw me.

"I was picking blueberries," I told her, no less surprised myself.

"At this time of night?" she asked, and before I could explain, her face went red and she said: "This is Johann."

I let go of the baskets, which had grown very heavy in my hands, said "hey," to Johann (for that's what people say in Sweden), and found Bibi gone.

"Come on," she was calling to me from outside, "come on home!"

So I said "hey," again, and ran after her.

On the way home, Bibi stopped suddenly and said: "Swear you won't tell anyone about Johann." And when I didn't answer at once, she warned me: "I'll leave you alone in the forest if you don't."

Alone in the forest with a troll behind every tree? I heaved a sigh and, willy-nilly, agreed.

“You mean it’s taken you all this time to fill your baskets?” asked Leo, who was waiting for me at the door. Maybe she had become worried about me after all, and was sorry she had left me in the forest.

“And where are the baskets?”

Only then did I remember them. A whole day’s work gone! But I had sworn to Bibi and couldn’t go back on it, so I said nothing.

I still ran into Johann a few times after that; once or twice in the forest, and once right near our house, where he “just happened” to be passing.

“How’s Bibi?” he asked.

“She’s fine,” I said.

“Please ask her to come out,” he begged.

But it appeared Bibi didn’t want to see him. When I went back to Johann and told him, he was very silent for a moment. Then he put his hand in his pocket and produced a little ring with a blue stone.

“Give it to Bibi to remember me by,” he told me, but then changed his mind. “No,” he said, smiling at me, “you take it.” He put it in my hand and went away.

And that was the last time I saw him.

Night thoughts

"Leo," I said one night, lying in bed and unable to sleep, "do you believe the war will ever end?"

I didn't think of the war by day, because our life in Sweden was peaceful and safe. We had been made to feel welcome at school in Stockholm, and all the kids wanted to be our friends. As refugees, we were nothing special, because Stockholm was full of refugees. But most of them came from other countries of Europe, and not many Danish refugees had come to the capital.

It was at night before falling asleep that the thoughts came.

"Leo," I said again, a bit louder, "do you think the war will ever end?" I was afraid she had fallen asleep. But she hadn't. Maybe Leo, too, had thoughts coming to her at night.

"Sure," she said at last. "It's just a matter of time. The Germans are getting a proper beating. It says so in the papers every day."

"So what will the papers write about when the war is over?"

"The things that worry you!" said Annette, laughing. I thought she had gone to sleep long ago. "Me, I've got a real worry," Annette went on: "Swedish grammar. I just can't make it out. If we don't go back to Denmark soon, I'll drop out of school." "Also," she added after a pause, "I'm worried about Collie. I wish I knew what's happened to him." Collie was Annette's dog, and she missed him. She missed all the animals she had left behind in Denmark. And thinking of them, Annette went to sleep.

"Leo," I whispered, "are you asleep?"

"Yes," she said.

"Tell me about Vejko and Sejpo," I begged.

Vejko and Sejpo were twins in Leo's class. They were from Finland, and all the kids were afraid of them because they wore long knives in their belts. They were prepared to use them, too. Leo was the only one who liked them. She also liked telling me about them, and about the Finnish people, and how brave they were. They had been through many wars. They had fought against the Russians and the Swedes, who had both tried to take parts of their country away from them. And having had to fight so often, the Finns had become a tough, stubborn and courageous people. Vejko and Sejpo didn't know whom they hated more, the Russians or the Germans. As for Jews, they had never met any, because there were only very few Jews in Finland. They did know that they had fought bravely in all of Finland's wars.

Jewish soldiers? I couldn't imagine such a thing. Could Leo? But Leo didn't answer.

"Leo," I begged, "please talk to me a bit."

But Leo had fallen asleep as well.

I sighed, said my "Shema Yisrael" night prayer, and then there was nothing to do but let the thoughts come...

Jewish refugees. We used to meet others like us in the tiny synagogue on Sabbaths and holidays. German Jews who had come to Denmark before the war, some of them who were learning to be farmers so they could go to *Eretz Israel* and join a kibbutz. Polish Jews who had lost all their families, or Sigrid who lived next door to us. She and her family were the only Norwegian Jews I knew. Sigrid was from a town called Trondheim. She told me proudly that theirs was the northernmost synagogue in the world. I liked hearing her talk, because Norwegian is sort of a singsong language, and every sentence sounds as though it has a question mark at the end. But some of the things she talked about made me feel bad.

The Germans had invaded Norway on the same day as Denmark. Unlike Denmark, though, Norway did fight the German attackers, but were soon forced to surrender.

The King escaped to England. The Germans appointed a Norwegian Nazi to rule over the country for them. His name was Quisling, and he ruled with such harshness and cruelty that his name has become another word for "traitor" in every language.

There were not many Jews in Norway. Some of them managed to escape across the border into Sweden, like Sigrid's family. The others were sent to their death in the camps.

And then I could think no longer, and the bad dream came: The Germans were hunting us. I was running and running, until I woke up, and was so tense and anxious that I couldn't get back to sleep at all.

We were like wild plants. Like dandelions. A wind blows and poof! – scatters us every which way. Like little parachute jumpers. Sometimes with a sunshade over our heads, sometimes an umbrella. Depending on the wind and the weather.

And so the months passed and became a year, then more months, and the Germans were losing on every front, and day by day it became clearer that soon the war would end.

Granny arrives

One day, very near the war's end, we received a letter saying that Granny was in Sweden. She had been in a group of people released from the German concentration camp of Theresienstadt.

The Nazis had set up Theresienstadt in Czechoslovakia as a "model" camp and used it for show. Conditions there were a little better than in other camps. Yet most Jews did not remain there for long, since it was a transfer camp and from there most of the prisoners were sent on to the death camps.

Except for the prisoners from Denmark. The Danish authorities and the Danish Red Cross did their best to look after their Jewish citizens, even after they had been deported. They sent parcels of clothes and food. They insisted on visiting the camp to see the conditions, and most important, they got the Germans to agree that the Jews from Denmark should stay in the camp and not be transferred.

What is more, they even managed, later, to do what no one else had, with the help of the Swedish Red Cross. They made the Germans let go of Jews they had captured. And so, a few weeks before the war in Europe ended, all the 450 Danish Jews in Theresienstadt were freed, and sent to Sweden. Among them was our Granny.

(The Germans knew they were losing the war and soon all their terrible crimes would be discovered. Maybe they believed that if they freed some prisoners, their punishment would be lighter.)

Granny, of course, wanted to join us in Stockholm at once, but she still had to wait a bit. Many of the people returning from Theresienstadt were ill, some of them with contagious diseases. The Swedish government therefore kept them apart in a special hospital camp to nurse them back to health, and to prevent their diseases spreading to others.

And then, at last, Granny was with us. Oh, how I had missed her! How I had waited to see her again! She looked even smaller than I remembered her. And there was another change. Her eyes, which had always been full of laughter, were so sad. They had seen so many horrors, that I looked in vain for the old smile in them.

I didn't know about the horrors at first. On the contrary, I thought Granny must have liked being in the camp, because everyone there spoke German like herself. I asked her about it, but for a long time Granny refused to talk about the camp at all. Only later, bit by bit, did she start telling us what had happened, speaking in her own special mishmash of German with a few Danish words.

Granny's story

They had been taken by ship from Copenhagen to Germany and then by train to Theresienstadt, first the Jews who had been arrested on the night of Rosh Hashanah and then all the others who hadn't managed to escape to Sweden, among them the Chief Rabbi. There were also some who had been caught by the Nazis when trying to get to the coast and the fishing boats.

Granny and other prisoners from Denmark in the camp received parcels of food and clothes from Denmark, which saved them from dying of hunger or cold. Their families could write to them. We had written to Granny, too, and she had received our letters and parcels. We had also received postcards from her.

Granny told us about the time the visitors from the Danish Foreign Ministry and Red Cross had come to see the camp, and how hard the Germans had tried to fool them. Before the visit, they had painted the buildings. They had planted grass and trees and made a children's playground, and sent away all the sick people from the camp. They had moved the Danish Jews to less crowded quarters, and had warned everyone not to tell the visitors anything about what life in the camp was really like. Anyone who would just give a hint of the truth would be sent to a death camp the following day.

That's how the Germans used the Jews from Denmark, trying to deceive the world.

Suddenly, one day, Granny and all the other Jews from Denmark were gathered outside the camp, and they saw a row of white buses standing there. The Danish and Swedish Red Cross had sent them. They were ordered to get on, and the buses started driving through Germany. It was a defeated Germany they saw, bombed and burned and ruined by years of war. They drove a long way until they reached Denmark. From there they were taken across to Sweden by ship.

Granny stopped talking. It was as though she still couldn't believe she was back with all of us again. She had been saved, and of course she was glad about it, but the horror of what had happened remained with her all her life. She could not talk about that. She never told us about life in the camp itself. Even in this "model" camp, the prisoners suffered terribly.

I realized there were many things about this war that I did not know and never would. But I also realized that I couldn't just think of forests and lakes while other people were suffering so much.

Goodbye to Mrs. Bluestone

The war was nearly over. Soon we would return to Denmark.

"Please," I asked Mama, "can we go to visit Mrs. Bluestone?" I hadn't seen her for almost two years, and now I wanted to say goodbye to her.

"All right," said Mama, "but let's first call her up on the phone. The Swedes are orderly people. They have their days all planned, and I don't think they like surprises."

We went by bus and trolley from our suburb to the center of town. Stockholm is a beautiful city, surrounded by water. It has a great many trees and flowers and everything is very clean. The nearer we got to Mrs. Bluestone's, the narrower the streets became. The houses stood close together here, with no room for trees at all. This was the old city of Stockholm, where Mrs. Bluestone lived.

"Funny," I thought to myself, "I noticed none of these things last time."

Mrs. Bluestone sat in a rocking chair in her dark living room, embroidering a cushion.

"How nice of you to come and say goodbye to me," she said. "Please sit down."

There was a plate on the table with pink marzipan cookies filled with whipped cream and a cup of cocoa for me. How had Mrs. Bluestone known that those were my favorite cookies? Or maybe they were her favorite as well?

"Why do you stand there dreaming, Maya?" Mama asked. "Why don't you come and sit down?"

Mrs. Bluestone smacked her lips, and all of a sudden I noticed she had the same sort of smile in her eyes as Granny used to have.

"It's been such a long time since I was here," I said. I crossed the room to the large curtain. I looked for the broken china swallow, but the windowsill was empty.

"What's the matter?" asked Mama anxiously. Did she think I would burst into tears again like last time?

"Nothing," I told her.

"Mrs. Bluestone," I asked, "why do you keep all the curtains closed? Don't you ever open them?"

"The light hurts my eyes," she explained. "But once in a great while I do open them, and then..." she paused for a moment, "then there is always some surprise."

I quickly took off the little ring with the blue stone Johann had given me, and put it on the windowsill where the swallow had been. I was sure Johann would understand. Then I went and sat down at the table.

After a while, when we got up to leave, I felt I had not just gotten fatter from all those marzipan cookies, I had also grown much older and wiser as well. There was a mirror in the hall, and I looked into it to see the change. But eyes don't always see everything.

Back to Denmark

And then the war was really over.

Peace. A feeling of happiness and relief! Everything was possible, everything permitted. The borders were open. But a whole, wonderful world had been destroyed, and could never be rebuilt. Millions of people had been killed, and a third of the Jewish people had been brutally murdered. What had happened would never be forgotten.

Those of Europe's Jews who had survived were now trying to find their way back to life. For some, that meant going to *Eretz Israel*, the country where three years later, the State of Israel would be born. For some, it meant wandering all over Europe to search for their lost families. And for some, it meant staying in the country that had given them refuge.

We ourselves, like most Danish Jews, went back to Denmark. We found our house as we had left it. Not a brick wrenched loose, not a window smashed. Almost everywhere else in Europe, returning Jews found their homes had been taken over by others, or had been broken into and everything of value stolen. But our house was untouched. The authorities and neighbors had taken care of the homes that the Jews had left, and looked after them till the owners came back.

Only our garden had changed. Everything had run wild. It looked like a jungle. The grass had grown almost to the height of a man, and all the paths had disappeared.

We only stayed in the village for a few months. Then we moved to Copenhagen and began a new life.

Afterword

In 1968, on the twenty-fifth anniversary of the rescue of Denmark's Jews, a group of Danish underground members was invited to come on a visit to Israel. They went to kibbutzim and met with people who had first learned to be farmers in Denmark. They visited Yad Vashem, the World Holocaust Remembrance Center. They were guests of honor at the festive opening of a new school in Jerusalem, the "Denmark School," and a new public square, "Denmark Square." Wherever they went, people received them with love and admiration.

By that time, I was living in Israel myself, and I talked to one member of the group, Mrs. Thomsen, who had come on this visit with two of her sons. Her husband had been an innkeeper on the coast, and he had smuggled Jews in his boat across the sea to Sweden. He was a member of the resistance. One day, he was arrested by the Germans and never returned.

I asked Mrs. Thomsen: "How come that in all Europe only you, the people of Denmark, came to the aid of the Jews? What made you do it?"

Mrs. Thomsen looked surprised.

"It was the obvious thing to do," she said, as if she didn't see the point of my question. "What we can't understand is why all the others didn't do the same."